AIR FRYER COOKBOOK

Step By Step Guide For Healthy, Easy And Delicious Air Fryer Recipes

John Carter

© Copyright 2018 by John Carter - All rights reserved.

This document is geared towards providing exact and reliable information in regards to the topic and issue covered. The publication is sold with the idea that the publisher is not required to render accounting, officially permitted, or otherwise, qualified services. If advice is necessary, legal or professional, a practiced individual in the profession should be ordered.

- From a Declaration of Principles which was accepted and approved equally by a Committee of the American Bar Association and a Committee of Publishers and Associations.

In no way is it legal to reproduce, duplicate, or transmit any part of this document in either electronic means or in printed format. Recording of this publication is strictly prohibited and any storage of this document is not allowed unless with written permission from the publisher. All rights reserved.

The information provided herein is stated to be truthful and consistent, in that any liability, in terms of inattention or otherwise, by any usage or abuse of any policies, processes, or directions contained within is the solitary and utter responsibility of the recipient reader. Under no circumstances will any legal responsibility or blame be held against the publisher for any reparation, damages, or monetary loss due to the information herein, either directly or indirectly.

Respective authors own all copyrights not held by the publisher.

The information herein is offered for informational purposes solely, and is universal as so. The presentation of the information is without contract or any type of guarantee assurance.

The trademarks that are used are without any consent, and the publication of the trademark is without permission or backing by the trademark owner. All trademarks and brands within this book are for clarifying purposes only and are the owned by the owners themselves, not affiliated with this document.

Table of Contents

CHAPTER 1 WHAT IS AIR FRYER? 1

CHAPTER 2 CONVERTING RECIPES 5

CHAPTER 3 HOW TO COOK FROZEN FOOD IN THE AIR FRYER 11

CHAPTER 4 HOW DOES AIR FRYER HELP IN DIETING AND WEIGHT LOSS? 13

CHAPTER 5 AIR FRYER RECIPES 23

CHAPTER 6 BREAD AND BREAKFAST 51

CHAPTER 7 MAIN MEALS 59

CHAPTER 8 DESSERTS AND SWEETS 80

CHAPTER 9 SOUP 99

CHAPTER 1
WHAT IS AIR FRYER?

An air fryer is a kitchen machine that cooks by circling hot air around the food. A mechanical fan courses the hot air around the food at fast, preparing the nourishment and delivering a fresh layer through the Maillard impact.

Conventional browning techniques prompt the Maillard impact by entirely submerging sustenance in hot oil. The air fryer works then again by covering the coveted food in a thin layer of oil while circling air warmed up to 200 °C to give vitality and start the response. By doing this, the machine can broil sustenance like potato chips, chicken, angle, steak, French fries or cakes while utilizing in the vicinity of 70% and 80% less oil than a conventional profound fryer.

Most air fryers accompany adjustable temperature, and clock handles that take into account more precise cooking. Nourishment is cooked in a cooking container that sits on a dribble plate. The container and its substance must occasionally be shaken to guarantee even oil scope; a few models achieve this by consolidating a sustenance fomenter that continually stirs the nourishment amid the cooking procedure while others require the client to play out the errand physically.

Air fryers are alluring for their benefit, security, and medical advantages. A chip fry for gold, with its open best, can without much of a stretch enable hot beads of cooking oil to escape or sprinkle out on the client, which isn't conceivable with an air fryer. Routinely broiled foods are likewise significantly higher in caloric substance, because of the oil retention confident in their arrangement. While proficient gourmet experts have expressed that air fryers complete a great job of making more advantageous copies of pan-fried nourishments, it is likewise, for the most part, concurred that the taste and consistency are not indistinguishable.

How Air Fryer Work?

Air-fryers are independent, windowsill convection stove (so oven with a fan inside), however, with a vertical primer: The fan blows down from the highest point of the gadget through an electric warming component. Wind current begins at best, warms up, at that point surges onto and around your nourishment through a work cooking container, lastly down to a molded dribble plate that recycles the air back to the best. The foodis then suspended amidst this wind current.

That work basket, incidentally, kinda-sorta resembles a profound rotisserie basket,and it's presumably where they got the name. In any case, there's no oil store or anything like that. Indeed, in spite of Philips' claims that you can "broil, barbecue, heat or meal utilizing a tablespoon or less of oil," a few formulas require no oil, or 2 tablespoons, or more. It depends.

Convection stoves and air fryers are fundamentally the same as far as how they cook sustenance, however air fryers are by and large littler than convection broilers and radiate less warmth. Comparable outcomes can be accomplished by utilizing special air crisper plate and placing them under the grill.

The idea behind air fryers is more advantageous, as it aims to bring down fat in cooking. Consolidating hot air, somewhat like a fan appliance, and a little measure of oil, the way they cook,is world-classand far from deep fat fryers which submerge the sustenance in the fat and heap on the calories. However, it's essential to get the correct air fryer as poor ones can abandon you with saturated, tasteless sustenance at the base of the machine – and now and then all through – and you can likewise end up with a device that is hard to work or clean.

Tips for Using an Air Fryer

Shake it.

Make absolute to open the air fryer and shake sustenance around as they "broil" in the machine's crate—littler nourishments like French fries and chips can pack. For best outcomes, pivot them each 4-10 minutes.

Try not to pack.

Nourishing a lot of room so the air can course viable; that is the thing that gives you new outcomes. Our test kitchen cooks swear by the air fryer for bites and little groups.

Give foods a squelch.

Delicately splash foods with acooling shower or include a tad of oil to guarantee they don't adhere to the crate.

Keep it dry.

Pat nourishments dry before cooking (if they are marinated, for instance) to abstain from splattering and abundance smoke. Likewise, when preparing high-fat nourishments, like chicken wings, make a point to discharge the fat from the base machine occasionally.

Ace other cooking strategies.

The air fryer isn't only to fry; it's fantastic for other robust cooking techniques like preparing, simmering and flame broiling, as well. Our test kitchen additionally cherishes to utilize the machine for cooking salmon!

CHAPTER 2
CONVERTING RECIPES

Converting From Traditional Recipes

You can utilize your air fryer to cook recipes that have guidelines for preparing in the grill. Since the heat noticeable all around fryer is more exceptional than a standard stove, diminish the proposed temperature by 24°F – 40°F and cut the time by approximately 20%. In this way, if a formula calls for cooking at 400°F for 20 minutes, air-sear at 370°F for around 16 minutes.

If you envision that you're cooking a dish supper for Sunday lunch. You have intended to make broil chicken with cook potatoes and vegetables. You would typically steam the vegetables in a skillet and afterward cook the chicken and the potatoes together in the stove; You would then complete dish chicken on the flame broil to fresh up the chicken and vegetables. In any case, now you have an Airfryer and after that exclusive drawback is that it is littler than the space you have in the stove however everything else is fundamentally the same. You would cook the chicken and potatoes together, but since the Airfryer goes about as the prepared, flame broiled and southern style across the board implies that there is less work and less oil included. You can put your chicken and potatoes similarly, at that point you would consist of the oil (however significantly less), and after that, it would cook uniformly and afterward you can serve it.

That chicken and potatoes that would, as a rule, take an hour and a half in the stove will take only 44 minutes in the

AIR FRYER COOKBOOK

Airfryer. Add to this that as opposed to splashing the potatoes with a considerable measure of oil to make them fresh you merely require a tablespoon of olive oil for every individual that you are cooking for.

So anticipate that Airfryer cooking will be straightforward and not as troublesome as the way you cook now, so it is a pleasant cooking experience.

Converting from Packaged Foods Directives

A similar manage applies to arranged sustenance that you may purchase at the supermarket. If a pack of solidified French fries proposes cooking in thegrill at440°F for 18 minutes, air sear the chips at 400°F and begin checking them at 14 minutes, making sure to shake the crate more than once amid the cooking procedure to enable the chips to darker uniformly.

Using Airfryer to prepare food from packaged food institutions would propel you to wind up testing a great deal to get things right. For instance, few recipes you will discover doesn't require any oil whatsoever, yet a few if you take them to an oil-free formula they can taste shocking. Be that as it may, generally speaking, you should hope to decrease the fat by around 64%.

In case you're an aficionado of KFC Chicken, Chicken Cordon Bleu or Chicken Schnitzel then you will love the oil-free forms for the Airfryer. They suggest a flavor like something that has been crisped and rotisserie when in certainty it has been breaded and made in a considerably more advantageous way. Expect experimentation however and have a fabulous time formula testing. Our Airfryer French Fries, for instance, took us 3 years to culminate them,and now our meals wouldn't be the same without them!

You can utilize your air fryer to cook formulas that have directions for preparingon the stove. Since the warmth, noticeable all around fryer is more extreme than a standard grill, diminish the proposed temperature by 24°F – 40°F and cut the time by approximately 20%. In this way, if a formula calls for cooking at 400°F for 20 minutes, air-broil at 370°F for around 16 minutes.

Converting to Different Sized Air-Fryers

Bigger air fryers can make life somewhat less demanding, particularly in case you're cooking for at least 4 individuals. Since the bushels in these air fryers are more significant, you can prepare more sustenance at one time and don't need to prepare the nourishment in clusters as determined in a considerable lot of these formulas.Merely recall not to over-fill the air fryer container, since that will directly back off the general cooking time and result in sustenance that is not as fresh as you'd like them to be. What's more, some bigger air fryers with more power may cook food marginally speedier than littler, bring down wattage air fryers. This won't be a unique distinction, yet may spare you 2 or 3 minutes on a few formulas. Similarly, as with everything you cook noticeable all around thefryer, it bodes well to pull open the air fryer combine and check the nourishment as they prepare. That way, you'll maintain a strategic distance from over-cooking anything.

People purchase air fryers primarilybecause they loath to (or have room schedule-wise to, or know how to) cook and a few

AIR FRYER COOKBOOK

people just need their broiled treats to be less greasy. The central possibly threatening part is that hurried edibles don't assist with directions for air fryer cooking.

Conversion is a frightening term, yet what's required is entirely straightforward. Air fryers will cook sustenance quicker than an ordinaryoven and needs shaking (shrimp, fries) like a deep fryer does, or flipping and blending, as stove guidelines do.

For impeccability, the readied, covered nourishment is showered with somewhat olive or canola oil, for greatest firmness. Try not to shower a pizza, at all!

Biggerair fryers cook sustenance speedier. Congestion of food anticipates wind current, which backs off cooking time. Moreover, nourishment that is stuffed may not end up noticeably fresh. Instead, it can rise out of your air fryer spongy and baffling.

A 4qt air fryer cooks 2fold the measure of nourishment as a 3qt. The bigger fryer can cook a whole chicken, roast different sustenances on the double and leave space for remains. Ultimately, a 4qt air fryer is basically superior esteem.

Apparently, there are times when a 3qt fryer might be more appropriate. On the off chance that you are cooking for just single or 2 individuals, a 3qt fryer could be perfect. This is particularly valid if you don't need scraps and are not anticipating facilitating extra individuals for future dinners. A 3qt air fryer is additionally better when counter space is constrained. Those on a financial plan may consider the 3qt air fryer as they tend to be more affordable than their more prominent partners.

CHAPTER 3
HOW TO COOK FROZEN FOOD IN THE AIR FRYER

Most pre-arranged foods cook speedier and at higher temperatures than are prescribed for stove warming. When you have changed over and prepared couple, you will have the best of it.

If you have ever managed a conventional oil fryer sometime recently, you know how muddled they can be. Having a hot vat of oil to profound sear your sustenance in can make a wide range of splatters in your kitchen. It can likewise be risky managing hot oil. It isn't phenomenal for individuals who possess oil fryers to get small consumes when oil dots or splatters out of the holder.

In spite of the fact that an advanced profound fryer is intended to dodge splatters, you have to broil legitimately to keep your nourishments from drenching a great deal of oil. Unless you utilize a conventional profound fryer that accompanies an indoor regulator to enable you to get the correct temperature, you may wind up getting oily nourishments. The inordinate oil can be destructive. Then again, air fryers give that same broiled freshness to your sustenance, without suffocating your nourishment in greasy oil.

One way recommended for cooking solidified nourishments in your fryer is utilizing your microwave to defrost it out first before you broil it. That will help abbreviate the critical cooking time that your beforehand solidified sustenance

AIR FRYER COOKBOOK

should be in the fryer. It will likewise help expel a portion of the dampness from your solidified nutrition with the goal that it can get decent and fresh in the fryer.

If you will be tossing some solidified meat, veggies, French fries, angle sticks, or potato tots straight into the air fryer, simply remember that they will require a more drawn out time fricasseeing, on the off chance that you didn't defrost them first.

Here Are Some Tips:

- Try not to utilize microwave warming bearings with an air fryer.

- Try not to utilize stove cooking headings as imprinted on the bundle.

- Do shake the bushels as in a profound fryer, or flip the sustenance as you would in a stove.

- Do splash the sustenance with a touch of cooking oil to ensure it crisps.

- You can fill a sustenance safe spritz bottle with your most loved oil. This is said to be better for nonstick surfaces, also.

CHAPTER 4
HOW DOES AIR FRYER HELP IN DIETING AND WEIGHT LOSS?

Dieting or slimming, whatever you call it, is a testing venture, however, it's justified regardless of the exertion. You may feel like you're stuck eating celery sticks and fat-free sustenances and think about whether you'll ever have the capacity to eat something that tastes great again. Are there approaches to appreciate the nourishment you cherish and still stay with your eating regimen?

Possibly you've known about an air fryer and are interested to find out about this progressive kitchen machine. Would it be able to help you with your eating fewer carbs and Weight reduction travel? What are some low-calorie air fryer suppers? What sorts of stable things can the air fryer cook? Is it conceivable to appreciate fricasseed sustenances without all the fat and calories?

In light of Rapid Air Technology, air fryers blow superheated air to cook sustenances that are customarily singed in oil. Regardless of whether you need to make fish sticks and French fries, chicken or even doughnuts, atmosphere that is up to 200 degrees' Celsius starts of course, forming a cooked, fresh surface.

In only 10 to 12 minutes, for example, you can cook a bunch of fries, utilizing significant portion of a spoonful of oil. Furthermore, that is only the start. From cakes to chunks, burgers to steaks, nourishments can be quickly cooked to accomplish similar outcomes when singing, toasting, heating or simmering.

The idea of Air fryerswas at first planned as a more secure, more straightforward technique for searing nourishments, and also diminishing oil-container fires and related wounds. Be that as it may, is this machine more beneficial?

Scientists found that air searing altogether decreased dampness and oil take-up. As far as free unsaturated fats, peroxide esteems and other physicochemical changes, specialists detailed more noteworthy changes in the oil removed from conventional searing techniques, in contrast with air fricasseeing. By and large, scientists presumed that utilizing an air-fryer is, indeed, a more beneficial strategy.

One critical thing to note is the likelihood of expanded free radicals. Regardless of whether little oil is utilized the kind of oil, the temperature, the nourishment that has been cooked and air circulation all impacts the arrangement of free radicals. In case you're a devotee of air browning, in any event, utilize oils that don't oxidize effortlessly, for example, coconut oil.

Before you hop for satisfaction, be that as it may, we have a deplorable yet to include. When taking a gander at the 10,000-foot view, it's smarter to move far from "broiled" sustenances, regardless of whether they're not dug in oil. By the day's end, the foods that air-browning aficionados float towards aren't the most beneficial choices.

As somebody who strives to get thinner and cook sound sustenances, we pondered on similar things. This is what we found about air fryers and Weight reduction. Ideally, the responses to these inquiries can help you on your counting calories and Weight reduction travel.

How Does an Air Fryer Help?

One of the skirmishes of eating fewer carbs is being confined to specific nourishments, especially if those sustenances don't taste great. Entirely disposing of carbs, desserts, singed sustenances, or other delicious things is troublesome and frequently abandons you longing for the things you're endeavoring to stay away from. This makes individuals more inclined to "swindling" on their eating routine and overindulging in unfortunate sustenances.

Cross the thresholdin the air fryer. This kitchen machine gives you the chance to appreciate some of your most loved nourishments, yet healthier. Things like potato chips and French fries cook to fresh, fulfilling flawlessness in an air fryer with practically zero oil and included fat. Changing the way, you prepare nourishments encourages you tostay with your eating regimen and Weight reduction design without giving up the kind of proper sustenance.

Air fryers are a speedy and straightforward approach to cook sustenance at home, where you control precisely what you're eating. They cook an assortment of foodsactively with next to zero oil. This settles on them an excellent decision for individuals who are taking a shot at getting more fit or need to eat substantial suppers. Hence, numerous thinning clubs suggest cooking with an air fryer.

Low-Calorie Meals

Air fryers can cook a wide assortment of sustenances, including chicken, angle, steak, vegetables, pastries, and that's only the tip of the iceberg. Dinners arranged noticeable all around fryer have a tendency to bring down calorie than conventional cooking strategies in light of the fact that the air fryer enables you to accomplish remarkable outcomes with insignificant oil.

Comprehensive Items to Cook in an Air Fryer

It's a snap to cook sound sustenances in an air fryer. A fun aspect concerning this kitchen machine is that it's anything but complicated to explore different avenues regarding and attempt new things. Here are a couple of opinions of sound sustenances that cook well in an air fryer:

- Broiled corn
- Prepared potatoes
- Sweet potato chunks
- Banana chips
- Firm Brussels grows
- Prepared eggs
- Jalapeno poppers
- Cooked carrots
- Vegetable variety

- Green beans with garlic sauce

- Kale chips

- Cooked chickpeas

- Flame broiled pineapple

- Egg and veggie frittata without hull – Season with somewhat salt and pepper and cook in scaled-down pie searches for gold high protein breakfast.

Crab cakes

Burgers – After turning the patties, include a cup of cheddar for whatever is left of the cooking time for a cheeseburger; the cheddar will dissolve onto the patty as it completes the process of cooking.

Chicken quesadillas

Nectar ginger salmon – Marinate salmon in soy sauce, squeezed orange, nectar, minced garlic, minced ginger, and scallions. Prepare at 400 degrees for 9 minutes.

Chicken Parmesan – So tasty you don't miss the breading.

Chicken strips – Dip in egg, at that point daintily bread with Panko pieces. Spritz with olive oil and prepare for 30 minutes at 400 degrees.

Parmesan crusted tortellini

Seared shrimp – Lightly bread, at that point cook to fresh flawlessness and present with mixed drink sauce.

AIR FRYER COOKBOOK

Pork hacks – Marinate in fat-free Italian serving of mixed greens dressing for 2-3 hours, at that point heat for 14 minutes.

Stuffed chime peppers

Lemon pepper chicken – Season chicken, at that point delicately spritz it with olive oil to keep it delicate.

- Chicken wings
- Toasted pumpkin seeds
- Cauliflower tator tots

As should be apparent, there are numerous reliable alternatives with regards to cooking with an air fryer. A most loved substantial side dish is simmered vegetables. Essentially hurl bits of green with little olive oil, season as indicated by taste, and cook at 400 degrees for 8-14 minutes. Broccoli, asparagus, cauliflower, and different vegetables turn out fresh and delightful when cooked along these lines.

Organic product or vegetable chips are another top choice. Daintily cut bananas, carrots, apples, radishes, zucchini, or different products of the soil and place in a single layer broadcasting live fryer plate. Gently season with salt if wanted and heat until it becomes crispy.

Fried Foods with Less Fat and Fewer Calories

Numerous most loved sustenances are browned and loaded with fat, making them untouchable as indicated by most eating routine designs. Notwithstanding, with an air fryer, you can enjoy fresh browned sustenances without the blame. French fries, potato chips, fricasseed chicken, and more are significantly more advantageous when cooked in an air fryer. Appreciate the nourishments you cherish without destroying your eating regimen by changing the way you cook them.

Air fryers use around 80 percent less oil than conventional profound fat fricasseeing. For some broiled sustenances, you can even leave the oil off entirely. Next to zero oil implies that air browned nourishments have far fewer calories and less fat than their conventional partners. Explore different avenues regarding your most loved nourishments to perceive what tastes best to you.

An air fryer is an impressive expansion to the home of anybody endeavoring to get in shape or eat solid nourishment. It's practically no fat cooking technique brings about firm, wonderful broiled nourishments that are much lower in calories, and also extraordinary prepared and simmered sustenances. If there is need for you to appreciate excellent tasting nourishment without destroying your eating routine, an air fryer could be the appropriate response.

It's difficult to cook an assortment of low-calorie dinners and other sound things in an air fryer. Indeed, even fricasseed sustenances aren't beyond reach because of this progressive cooking technique. What are your most loved things to cook in an air fryer? Offer formulas or post any inquiries you have in the remarks.

Try not to deny yourself of all your most loved nourishments with an end goal to stay with a constrained eating routine. Appreciate sound nourishments that taste awesome by changing the way you cook them. Give your eating regimen,and Weight reduction travel a lift by exploring different avenues regarding low-calorie formulas in an air fryer.

Air Fryer and Low Carb

Humans love to feel incredible and look fantastic. For a few people, a low-carb or keto consume fewer calories areconventional method to accomplish this objective. Shockingly, diets like these are limited and may leave you inclining that you can't eat the nourishment you cherish. Are there approaches to keep on enjoying extraordinary tasting nourishments on a low-carb eat less?

Would it be conceivable to make great broiled sustenances that fit with a keto abstain from food? Does cooking at home make it less demanding to stay with an eating routine? Could an air fryer make low-carb nourishments more charming?

With an end goal to answer these inquiries and that's only the tip of the iceberg, researchers set out to take in more of solid low-carb eating and the way toward cooking with an air fryer.

Cooking food for a low-carb or keto abstain from food is trying on occasion. Specific ingredients are confined or forbidden which makes it hard to make the sustenances you cherish. An air fryer can help make things simpler in case you're attempting to take after a unique eating design.

Here are some ways an air fryer supplements a low-carb eat less:

- You can appreciate browned nourishments without the carbs

- It makes cooking at home speedier and less demanding

- Adaptable cooking alternatives keep things fascinating

- Enjoying Fried Foods on a Low-Carb Diet

Singed nourishments are famously undesirable and an improbable piece of any eating routine. Air fryers turn that around. Their progressive cooking technique enables you to accomplish firm, seared nourishments without overabundance oil. This makes it conceivable to appreciate seared nourishments while staying with an eating routine.

Pick a low-carb breading choice when searing sustenance for a keto count calories. Nut flours are a formidable choice for low-carb breading. For some additional surface, attempt finely hacking nuts as opposed to utilizing a nut flour. Splash or hurl sustenances with a saturated or monounsaturated cooking fat like avocado oil, coconut oil, or macadamia oil.

You can put singed sustenances you thought you'd abandoned the keto eating routine back on the menu with an air fryer.

CHAPTER 5
AIR FRYER RECIPES

APPETIZERS

Ricotta Balls with Basil

This Philips Airfryer recipe is a great appetizer for a revelry dinner, or any other occasion.

Ingredients

- 3 slices of stale white bread pepper, freshly ground
- 250 g of ricotta
- 15 g of finely chopped fresh basil
- 2 tablespoons of flour
- 1 separated egg
- 1 tablespoon of finely chopped chives

Guidelines

- Mix everything well together and add 1 tsp of salt and freshly ground pepper, as much as you'd like. After mixing everything, add the chives, the basil, as well as some orange peel.
- You'll be making the balls out of this mixture, so make sure it is well composed.

AIR FRYER COOKBOOK

- Make 20 portions out of the mixture and wet your hands to be able to roll them. Make ball shaped portions and leave them to rest.

- You should preheat your air fryer to 200º C.

- Prepare the bread crumbs out of the bread slices in one bowl, while beating the egg white in another.

- Roll each of the balls into the egg white, and then the bread crumbs.

- Fry the balls 10 by 10, each 10 for 8 minutes.

CHAPTER 5: AIR FRYER RECIPES

Air-Fried Beignets

These beignets are scrumptious all alone, yet you can influence chocolate to sauce or raspberry sauce to dress them up on the off chance that you like. To make a super simple and speedy raspberry sauce, mix some raspberry stick with 1 tablespoon of warm water. Thin it just to the consistency you like for plunging.

Ingredients

- A third-quarter filled glass tepid water (around 90°F)
- A quarter-filled glass sugar
- 1 profuse teaspoon dynamic dry yeast
- 3 ½ - 4 glasses useful flour
- A half-filled teaspoon salt
- 2 tablespoons unsalted margarine, room temperature and cut into little pieces
- 1 egg, softly beaten
- A half-filled glass dissipated drain
- ¼ container liquefied spread
- 1container confectioners' sugar
- Chocolate sauce or raspberry sauce, to plunge

25

AIR FRYER COOKBOOK

Guidelines

- Merge the tepid water, a squeezable amount of the sugar and the yeast in a bowl and let it cook for 4 minutes. It should foam a bit. If it doesn't foam, your yeast isn't dynamic, and you should begin again with new yeast.

- Consolidate 3½ measures of the flour, salt, 2 tablespoons of margarine and the rest of the sugar in a substantial bowl, or in the bowl of a stand blender. Include the egg, garnished drain and yeast blend to the pan and blended with a wooden spoon (or the oar connection of the stand blender) until the point when the mixture meets up in a sticky ball. Include somewhat more flour if essential to get the mixture to shape. Exchange the batter to an oiled bowl, cover with plastic wrap or a perfect kitchen towel and let it ascend in a warm place for no less than two hours or until the point when it has multiplied in mass. Longer is better for enhance advancement, and you can even give the mixture a chance to rest in the fridge overnight (merely make sure to convey it to room temperature before continuing with the formula).

- Roll the mixture out to ½-inch thickness. Cut the dough into rectangular or precious stone molded pieces. You can make the beignets any size you like. However, this formula will give you 24 (2-inch x 3-inch) rectangles.

- Pre-warm the air fryer to 340°F.

CHAPTER 5: AIR FRYER RECIPES

- Brush the beignets on the 2 sides with a portion of the softened spread and air-broil in groups at 340°F for 4 minutes, turning them over part of the way through if wanted. (They will darker on all sides without being flipped, yet flipping them will dark colored them all the more equally.)

- When the beignets are done, exchange them to a plate or preparing sheet and tidy with the confectioners' sugar. Serve warm with a chocolate or raspberry sauce.

AIR FRYER COOKBOOK

Baked Ricotta with Lemon and Capers

You could add an egg to this dish and get a puffier outcome - merely ensure you prepare the blend in a straight-sided skillet. To make formula somewhat lighter, you could utilize part-skim ricotta cheddar, yet you'll miss the extravagant lavishness of the cheddar. This is a canapé or bite, so go for the entire drain form and offer it to companions.

Ingredients

- 7-inch pie dish or cake container
- 1½ container entire drain ricotta cheddar or cheese
- Zest of 1 lemon, in plus more for savory
- 1 teaspoon finely hacked new rosemary
- Squeeze pulverized red pepper chips
- 2 washed tablespoons
- 2 tablespoons of additional virgin olive oil
- Salt and newly ground dark pepper
- 1 tablespoon ground Parmesan cheddar

Guidelines

- Pre-warm the air fryer to 380°F.
- Combine the ricotta cheddar or cheese, lemon get-up-and-go, rosemary, red pepper pieces, olive oil, salt and

CHAPTER 5: AIR FRYER RECIPES

pepper in a bowl and whisk together well. Exchange to a 7-inch pie dish and place noticeable all around fryer basket. You can utilize aluminum thwart sling to help with this by taking a long bit of aluminum thwart, collapsing it down the middle the long way twice until the point when it would seem that it is around 26-creeps by 3-inches. Place this under the pie dish and hold the finishes of the thwart to move the pie dish all through the air fryer crate. Tuck the finishes of the thwart next to the pie dish while it cooks noticeable all around afryer.

- Air-broil at 380°F for 8 to 10 minutes, or until the point when the best is pleasantly sautéed in spots.

- Expel from the air fryer and promptly sprinkle the Parmesan cheddar to finish everything. Sprinkle somewhat more olive oil to finish everything and include some naturally ground dark pepper and some lemon get-up-and-go as atopping. Serve warm with pita chips or crostini.

AIR FRYER COOKBOOK

Sizzling Air Fryer Turkey Fajitas Platter

You can likewise change this around to white meat you have remaining in your ice chest and you could even do it with extra hotdogs. Also, in light of the fact that it is hacked, prepared and tossed in you can return to putting your feet up or opening a container of wine.

Ingredients

- Philips Airfryer
- 6 Tortilla Wraps
- 100 g Leftover Turkey Breast
- 1 Large Avocado
- 1 Large Yellow Pepper
- 1 Large Red Pepper
- 1 Large Green Pepper
- ½ Small Red Onion
- 5 Tbsp Soft Cheese
- 3 Tbsp Cajun Spice
- 2 Tbsp Mexican Seasoning
- 1 Tsp Cumin
- Salt & Pepper

CHAPTER 5: AIR FRYER RECIPES

- Fresh Coriander

Guidelines

- Begin by cutting up your serving of mixed greens. Cleave your avocado into little wedges. Dice your red onion. Cut your peppers into thin cuts.

- Slash up your turkey breast into little pieces.

- Place the turkey, peppers and onions into a bowl and blend with every one of the seasonings alongside the delicate cheddar and afterward put in silver thwart and air broil for 20 minutes on 200c.

- To prevent your turkey from going dry you have to include dampness/fluid to it before you cook it. It's also important that you silver thwart it to again prevent it from going dry.

Spinach and Artichoke White Pizza

You can utilize your most loved locally acquired pizza mixture for this spinach artichoke white pizza formula

Ingredient

- Olive oil
- 3 mugs new spinach
- 2 cloves garlic, minced, partitioned
- 1 (6-to 8-ounce) pizza mixture ball
- ½ glass ground mozzarella cheddar
- ¼ glass ground Fontina cheddar
- ¼ glass artichoke hearts, coarsely hacked
- 2 tablespoons ground Parmesan cheddar
- ¼ teaspoon dried oregano
- Salt and crisply ground dark pepper

Guidelines

- Heat the oil in medium sauté container on the stovetop. Include the spinach and a significant portion of the minced garlic to the dish and sauté for a couple of minutes, until the point that the spinach has withered. Expel the sautéed spinach from the container and put it aside.

CHAPTER 5: AIR FRYER RECIPES

- Pre-warm the air fryer to 390°F.

- Cut out a bit of aluminum thwart an equal size from the base of the air fryer basket. Brush the thwart hover with olive oil. Shape the batter into a circle and place it over the thwart. Dock the mixture by puncturing it a few times with a fork. Brush the paste daintily with olive oil and move it into the air fryer container with the thwart on the base.

- Air-fry the plain pizza mixture for 6 minutes. Turn the mixture over, expel the aluminum thwart and brush again with olive oil, air-broil for an extra 4 minutes.

- Sprinkle the mozzarella and Fontina cheeses over the mixture. Top with the spinach and artichoke hearts. Sprinkle the Parmesan cheddar and dried oregano to finish everything and shower with olive oil. Lower the temperature of the air fryer to 340°F and cook for 8 minutes, until the point that cheddar has softened and is delicately caramelized. Season to taste with salt and new ground dark pepper.

Tandoori Chicken

Tandoori Chicken Recipe is a lip-smacking dry chicken dish from the Indian subcontinent, and it happens to be that one dish that a gathering or assembling just can't manage without. Chicken marinated in flavors till it gets the profound, dynamic look and taste, and from there on cooked in an Indian style.

Ingredients

- 4 Chicken legs
- For the first Marinade
- Ginger paste - 3 tsp
- Garlic paste - 3 tsp
- Salt to taste
- Lemon juice - 3 tbsp
- For the second Marinade
- Tandoori masala powder - 2 tbsp
- Roasted cumin powder - 1 tsp
- Garam masala powder - 1 tsp
- Red chili powder - 2 tsp
- Turmeric powder - 1 tsp
- Hung curd - 4 tbsp

CHAPTER 5: AIR FRYER RECIPES

- Orange food color - a pinch
- KasuriMethi - 2 tsp
- Black pepper powder - 1 tsp
- Coriander powder - 2 tsp

Guidelines

- Wash the chicken legs and make openings in them utilizing a sharp blade.
- Include the chicken in a bowl alongside the elements for the principal marinade.
- Blend well and keep aside for 15 minutes.
- Blend the elements for the second marinade and pour them over the chicken.
- Cover the bowl and refrigerate for no less than 10-12 hours.
- Line the bushel of the air fryer with aluminum foil.
- Pre warmth to 230 degrees C.
- Place the chicken on the bushel and air broil for 18-20 minutes, until somewhat scorched and cooked.
- Serve hot with Yogurt mint plunge and Onion rings

AIR FRYER COOKBOOK

Air Fryer Baked Garlic Parsley Potatoes

Air Fryer Baked Potato shrouded in a parsley garlic salt rub. You'll never eat a plain baked potato again!

In case you're here to figure out how to prepare a potato you're in the correct spot. The air fryer baked potatoes are such a great amount of superior to making a baked potato in the stove. When you put on the seasonings it just takes the potatoes to another level.

- **Mac and Cheese**

Ingredients:

- 2 cups of dry macaroni of your choice

- 2 cups of shredded cheddar cheese

- 1 tsp of corn starch

- 2 cups of heavy whipping cream

Guidelines

- Add the corn starch and half the cup of cheese in a bowl and mix them well with all the other ingredients.

- Add the mixture into the baking pan of your air fryer and cover with foil.

- Now, add the pan into the frying basket. Most of the air fryers have a bake setting. Choose if available.

CHAPTER 5: AIR FRYER RECIPES

- Cook the mixture for approximately 15 minutes, at 310 degrees.

- After 15 minutes, remove the foil and add the rest of the cheese.

- Continue the baking process for another 10 minutes, at the same temperature

Ingredients

- 3 Idaho or Russet Baking Potatoes
- 1-2 Tablespoons Olive Oil
- 1 Tablespoon Salt
- 1 Tablespoon Garlic
- 1 Teaspoon Parsley

Guidelines:

- Wash your potatoes and after that make air openings with a fork in the potatoes.

- Sprinkle them with the olive oil and seasonings; at that point rub the seasoning equitably on the potatoes.

- Once the potatoes are covered place them into the bushel for the Air Fryer and place into the machine.

- Cook your potatoes at 392 degrees for 35-40 minutes or until the point that fork delicate.

AIR FRYER COOKBOOK

- Top with your top picks. We cherish new parsley and sour cream

CHAPTER 5: AIR FRYER RECIPES

Air Fryer Falafel Balls

Air Fryer Falafel Balls are crunchy outwardly, delicate within, and idealize on plates of mixed greens or stuffed into a pita. Shower with custom made tahini dressing.

Ingredients

- 2 tablespoons olive oil
- 1/2 cup diced sweet onion
- 1/2 cup minced carrots
- 1/2 cup roasted salted cashews
- 1 cup rolled oats
- 2 cups cooked or 1, 15 ounce can-sealed chickpeas
- 2 tablespoon soy sauce
- juice of 1 fresh lemon
- 1 tablespoon flax meal
- 1 teaspoon each ground cumin and garlic powder
- 1/2 teaspoon turmeric

Guidelines

- In an extensive skillet, warm the olive oil on medium high warmth. Cook the onions and carrots until the point that they mollify, around 7 minutes, at that point exchange them to an expansive bowl.

AIR FRYER COOKBOOK

- Put the cashews and oats into your sustenance processor and crush until the point that you get a coarse dinner. Add that to the bowl with the veggies.

- Put the chickpeas into your sustenance processor with the soy sauce and lemon squeeze and puree until they're semi-smooth (a few pieces are thoroughly alright). You'll presumably need to stop and rub down the side a couple of times to get things moving. Exchange those to a similar bowl, at that point mix in the flax and flavors. Ensure everything is fused extremely well, and utilize a fork to squash up any enormous bits of chickpeas that you experience while you're mixing. It's fine in the event that you don't crush each and every chickpea. This formula is extremely lenient.

- Utilize your hands to make 12 falafel balls from the mixture, at that point organize them in a solitary layer in your air fryer bushel.

- Cook at 370 for 12 minutes, shaking following 8 minutes.

- Serve stuffed into a wrap or over plate of mixed greens with Magical Tahini Dressing.

CHAPTER 5: AIR FRYER RECIPES

Fried Green Tomatoes with Sriracha Mayo

This formula is best made in the late spring when tomatoes are in season, and most stores convey green vegetables (tomatoes precisely) or even better pick them right on time from your particular garden. A primary and decent approach to dress these up is to top each completed fricasseed tomato cut with some fresh crabmeat and shower the sriracha mayonnaise to finish everything.

Ingredients

- 3 green tomatoes
- Salt and newly ground dark pepper
- 1-third of container flour
- 2 eggs
- ½ container buttermilk
- 1 container of breadcrumbs
- 1 container of cornmeal
- New thyme sprigs or cleaved fresh chives
- Sriracha Mayo:
- ½ container mayonnaise
- 1 to 2 tablespoons hot sriracha sauce
- 1 tablespoon drain

AIR FRYER COOKBOOK

Guidelines

- Cut the tomatoes in ¼-inch cuts. Pat them dry with a cleanscullerycloth and season liberally with salt and pepper.

- Set up a digging station utilizing 3 shallow dishes. Place the flour in the main shallow bowl, consolidate the eggs and buttermilk in the second plate, and join the flour and cornmeal in the third recipe.

- Pre-warm the air fryer to 400°F.

- Dig the tomato cuts in flour to coat on the 2 sides. At that point dunk them into the 9egg blend lastly squeeze them into the breadcrumbs tocover all sides of the tomato.

- Splash or brush the air-fryer bushel with olive oil. Exchange 3 to 4 tomato cuts into the container and shower the best with olive oil. Air-broil the tomatoes at 400°F for 8 minutes. Flip them over, shower the opposite favor oil and air-fry for an extra 4 minutes until brilliant darker.

- While the tomatoes are cooking, make the sriracha mayo. Consolidate the mayonnaise, 1 tablespoon of the hot sriracha sauce and drain in a little bowl. Mix well until the point when the blend is smooth. Add more sriracha sauce to taste.

- At the point when the tomatoes are done, exchange them to a cooling rack or a platter fixed with paper towels, so the base does not get spongy. Before serving,

CHAPTER 5: AIR FRYER RECIPES

painstakingly stack the every one of the tomatoes into air fryer and air-broil at 340°F for 1 to 2 minutes to warm them go down.

- Serve the fried green tomatoes hot with the sriracha mayo as an afterthought. Season 1 final time with salt and naturally ground dark pepper and embellishment with sprigs of fresh thyme or hacked fresh chives.

Sockeye Salmon en Papillote with Potatoes, Fennel & Dill

Ingredients

- 2 to 3 fingerling potatoes, daintily cut ¼-inch thick
- ½ globule fennel, meagerly sliced ¼-inch thick
- 4 tablespoons spread, liquefied
- Salt and newly ground dark pepper
- New freshdill
- 2 (6-ounce) sockeye salmon filets
- 8 cherry tomatoes split
- Quarter-filled container dry vermouth (or white wine or fish stock)

Guidelines

- Pre-warm the stove (or air fryer) to 400°F.
- Heat a little pot of salted water to the point of boiling. Whiten the potato cuts for 2minutes until they merely begin to mollify marginally. Deplete and dry with a spotless kitchen towel.
- Cut out 2 expansive rectangles of material paper – around one 3-creep by 14-inches each. Hurl the potatoes, fennel, half of the dissolved spread, salt and newly ground dark pepper together in a bowl. Partition

CHAPTER 5: AIR FRYER RECIPES

the vegetables between the 2 bits of material paper, setting the vegetables on one portion of every rectangle. Sprinkle some crisp dill to finish everything.

- Place a filet of salmon on each heap of vegetables. Season the fish exceptionally well with salt and pepper. Hurl the cherry tomatoes to finish everything. Sprinkle the rest of the margarine over the fish. Separation the vermouth between the 2 bundles, showering it over the fish.

- Crease up every material square by first collapsing the rectangles into equal parts over the fish. Beginning at one corner, make a progression of straight overlays on the external edge of the squares to seal the edge together.

- Place the 2 bundles onto a heating sheet and prepare in the 400°F oven for 14 to 20 minutes. (Or then again, cook one bunch at any given moment noticeable all around fryer for 10 minutes each.) The bunch ought to be puffed up and marginally fried when thoroughly cooked. The fish should feel firm to the touch (you can frequently, deliberately, push on the fish through the paper).

- You can serve these primarily with the material paper efficiently slice open to uncover the internal parts, have your guests cut open the bundles at the table, or evacuate the material totally, exchanging the top-notch inner pieces to a plate. Sauce with somewhat more fresh dill.

Pickle-Brined Fried Chicken

This is a scrumptious singed chicken recipe that utilizes the saline solution left in the pickle jostle when you've completed every one of the pickles. This formula calls for legs, however, if you favor white meat, don't hesitate to substitute bone-in chicken bosoms.

Ingredients

- 4 chicken legs (bone-in and skin-on), cut into drumsticks and thighs (around 3½ pounds)
- Pickle juice from a 24-ounce jug of genuine dill pickles
- Half-filled glass of flour
- Salt and naturally ground dark pepper
- 2 eggs
- 2 tablespoons vegetable or canola oil
- 1 fine glass breadcrumbs
- 1 teaspoon salt
- 1 teaspoon typicallygrated dark pepper
- ½ teaspoon ground paprika
- ⅛ teaspoon cayenne pepper
- Vegetable or canola oil in a shower bottle

CHAPTER 5: AIR FRYER RECIPES

Guidelines

- Place the chicken in a shallow dish and pour the pickle squeeze over the best. Cover and exchange the chicken in the fridge to salt water in the pickle juice for 3 to 8 hours.

- When you are prepared to cook, expel the chicken from the fridge to give it a chance to come to room temperature while you set up a rigging station.Place the flour in a trivial dish and season well with salt and crisply ground dark pepper. Whisk the eggs and vegetable oil together in a moment shallow dish. In a third shallow dish, consolidate the breadcrumbs, salt, pepper, paprika and cayenne pepper.

- Pre-warm the air fryer to 370°F.

- Expel the chicken from pickle brackish water and tenderly dry it with a perfect kitchen towel. Dig each bit of chicken in the flour, at that point dunk it into the egg blend, lastly squeeze it into the breadcrumb blend to coat all sides of the chicken. Place the breaded chicken on a plate or preparing sheet and splash each piece done with vegetable oil.

- Air-broil the chicken in 2 clusters. Place 2 chicken thighs and 2 drumsticks into the air fryer bushel. Air-broil for 10 minutes. At that point, delicately turn the chicken pieces over and air broil for an additional 10 minutes. Expel the chicken pieces and let them lay on theplate – don't cover. Rehash with the second cluster

47

of chicken, air browning for 20 minutes, turning the chicken over part of the way through.

- Lower the temperature of the air fryer to 340°F. Place the central clump of chicken over the second group as of now in the crate and air broil for an extra 7 minutes. Warm and enjoy.

CHAPTER 5: AIR FRYER RECIPES

Air-Fried Turkey Breast with Maple Mustard Glaze

How awesome that you can cook a turkey bosom in your air fryer! That implies that you can prepare an extra heartin caseyou have a tremendous group for thanksgiving, or in case you're having a little gathering, you can air-broil your turkey and leave your stove accessible for all the side dishes. You'll need a considerable air fryer for this formula - no less than 4 quarts in themeasure. If you have alittle air fryer, you can attempt a boneless 3-pound turkey breast and cook it for around 30 –4 to 4 minutes

Ingredients

- 2 teaspoons olive oil
- 4-pound entire turkey bosom
- 1 teaspoon dried thyme
- ½ teaspoon drained sage
- ½ teaspoon smoked paprika
- 1 teaspoon salt
- ½ teaspoon newly ground dark pepper
- ¼ container maple syrup
- 2 tablespoon Dijon mustard
- 1 tablespoon butter

AIR FRYER COOKBOOK

Guidelines

- Pre-warm air fryer to 340°F.

- Brush the olive oil everywhere throughout the turkey bosom.

- Consolidate the thyme, sage, paprika, salt,and pepper and rub the outside and visible part of the turkey bosom with the zest blend.

- Exchange the prepared turkey bosom to the air fryer crate and air-fry at 340°F for 24 minutes. Turn the turkey bosom on its side and air-fry for an additional 12 minutes. Turn the turkey bosom on the contrary side and air-broil for an extra 12 minutes. The inside temperature of the turkey bosom should achieve 164°F when thoroughly cooked.

- While the turkey is air-frying, consolidate the maple syrup, mustard and spread in a little pan. At the point when the concocting time is, restore the turkey bosom to an upright position and brush the coating everywhere throughout the turkey. Air-broil for a last 4 minutes, until the point when the skin is pleasantly cooked and fresh. Give the turkey a chance to rest, approximately rose with thwart, for no less than 4 minutes before cutting and serving.

CHAPTER 6
BREAD AND BREAKFAST

Peach Crisp

Ingredients

- 4 cups of sliced peaches, frozen
- 3 Tablespoon sugar
- 2 Tablespoon Flour, white
- Teaspoon sugar, white
- 0.25 cup Flour, white
- 0.33 cup oats, dry rolled
- 3 tablespoon butter, unsalted
- 1 teaspoon cinnamon
- 3 tablespoon pecans, chopped

Guidelines

- In a bowl, mix the peaches with 3 Tbsp. sugar, 2 Tbsp. flour and 1 tsp. cinnamon. Pour into the Baking Pan.
- Place the Baking Pan into the Fry Basket.
- Secure the Fry Basket inside the Power Air Fryer XL.

AIR FRYER COOKBOOK

- Set time & temperature manually to 20 minutes at 300 degrees.

- Half way through cooking, give the peaches a stir.

- In a bowl mix the rest of the ingredients to make the crisp topping.

- When the time runs out on the peaches, remove the Fry Basket and top with the crisp topping.

- Place the Fry Basket back into the Power Air Fryer XL.

- Press the Power Button & adjust cooking time to 10 minutes at 310 degrees and Bake.

- When the crisp is done, let cool for 15 minutes. Serve with your favorite ice cream.

CHAPTER 6: BREAD AND BREAKFAST

Fish Tacos

Ingredients:

- 10 ounces of cod filet
- 1 cup of Panko
- 6 flour tortillas
- 1 cup of tempura batter
- 1 cup of cole slaw
- 0.5 cup of salsa
- 1 tsp of white pepper
- 0.5 cup of guacamole
- 2 tbsp of chopped cilantro
- 1 lemon cut into wedges
- Power XL Air Fryer

Guidelines:

- Make the tempura batter by mixing 1 cup of flour, 1 tbsp of cornstarch, and half a cup of seltzer water cold.
- Add some salt to the mixture, and make it smooth.
- Cut the Cod filets into long 2 oz pieces. After doing so, season each piece with pepper and salt.

- Use the previously made batter to cover the pieces. Dredge them in the panko.

- Add the pieces into the air fryer basket. If your air fryer comes with a French Fry setting, choose that button.

- The estimated frying time is 10 minutes. After 5 minutes, turn the pieces.

- Once they're ready, put a piece on a tortilla with guacamole, cole slaw, salsa, and a spritz of lemon juice. You can also add the chopped cilantro.

CHAPTER 6: BREAD AND BREAKFAST

Monte Cristo Sandwich

A Monte Cristo sandwich is a "French toasted ham and cheddar sandwich." It has the sweet taste of French toast with the salty kind of the ham and Swiss cheddar to make a truly divine blend. It's presented with powdered sugar and an organic product safeguard, yet there are such a large number of varieties of the sandwich that it's honestly up to you how you'd get a kick out of the chance to serve it.

Ingredients

- 1 egg for omelets
- 3 tablespoons creamer
- ¼ teaspoon vanilla concentrate
- 2piecesof sourdough, white or multigrain bread
- 2½ ounces cut Swiss cheddar
- 2ounces' cuts store ham
- 2 ounces cut store turkey
- 1 teaspoon margarine, dissolved
- Powdered sugar
- Raspberry stick, for serving

Guidelines

- Mix the egg, cream and vanilla flavor in a shallow bowl.

- Place the bread on the counter. Construct a sandwich with one cut of Swiss cheddar, the ham, the turkey and after that a moment cut of Swiss cheddar on one cut of the bread. Top with the other cut of dough and press down marginally to straighten.

- Pre-warm the air fryer to 340°F.

- Cut out a bit of aluminum thwart about an indistinguishable size from the bread and brush the thwart with dissolved margarine. Plunge the 2 sides of the sandwich into the egg hitter. Give the hitter a chance to drench into bread for around 30 seconds on each side. At that point put the sandwich on the lubed aluminum thwart and exchange it to the air fryer container. For additional frying, brush the highest point of the sandwich with thedissolved spread. Air-fry at 340°F for 10 minutes. Flip the sandwich over, brush with spread and air-broil for an extra 8 minutes.

- Exchange the sandwich to a serving plate and sprinkle with powdered sugar. Present with raspberry as an extra enjoyment.

CHAPTER 6: BREAD AND BREAKFAST

Pumpkin and Sunflower Seed Soft Bums Fruit Cake Air Fry Bread

Have you ever consider baking your homemade crisp bread? It's not a smart thought in light of the fact that, with your air fryer, you can accomplish more than heat a cake and basic dinners with fruits.

Ingredients

- 215 grams flour
- 30 grams sugar
- 100 grams of fresh milk)
- 30 grams of butter
- 1/3 egg
- 1 teaspoon of instant yeast
- 1 teaspoon of salt

Guidelines:

- Right off the bat, every one of the ingredients without butter ought to be combined. At the point when the blend's smooth and versatile, then add the butter spread at that point keep on mixing them.

- Now the bread ought to be sealed in 2 hours 45 minutes to have the batter twofold in measure. From that point onward, it ought to be secured with a top or stick wrap.

AIR FRYER COOKBOOK

Additionally, you ought to keep all the breeze from become scarce the bread.

- Here, the mixture ought to be separated into balls of 25 grams and rest them for around 10 minutes.

- Blend the egg yolk with drain or water to have the egg wash.

- Presently, you simply need to shape the blend into the ball and put them on the preparing paper. You can have an alternate shape as you need. From that point forward, cover them with egg wash above.

- From that point onward, the mixture needs sealing again in 45 minutes to have multiplied in measure and have every one of them in a warm condition.

- After about 45 minutes, take it out and splash them with a water to give additional dampness. At that point, heat them in the air fryer at 160 degrees C for 5 minutes.

- All things considered, you simply need to brush the bun with some margarine and appreciate it.

- While blending the ingredients, you ought to do until the point when they are not stickier but however, glossy and smooth. Likewise, please keep all the breeze from the mixture to be not dry them and you can accelerate the sealing time by a kitchen with hotter temperature

CHAPTER 7
MAIN MEALS

Black Cod with Grapes, Fennel, Pecans and Kale

Dark cod is otherwise called sablefish or butterfish. It's not quite of the cod family and not like cod in flavor or surface. It's rich and nutritious and has more sound omega-3 unsaturated fats than some other white fish.

Ingredients

- 2 (6-to 8-ounce) filets of dark cod (or sablefish)
- Salt and newly ground dark pepper
- Olive oil
- 1 container grapes, split
- 1 little knob fennel, cut ¼-inch thick
- ½ glass pecans
- 3 mugs of threadbare kale
- 2 teaspoons white balsamic vinegar or white wine vinegar
- 2 tablespoons additional virgin olive oil

Guidelines

- Pre-warm the air fryer to 400° F.

- Season the cod filets with salt and pepper and sprinkle, spread or shower a little olive oil to finish everything. Place the fish, introduction side up (skin side down), into the air fryer bushel. Air-broil for 10 minutes.

- At the point when the fish has got done with cooking, evacuate the filets to a side plate and freely tent with thwart to rest.

- Hurl the grapes, fennel and pecans in a bowl with a shower of olive oil and season with salt and pepper. Include the grapes, fennel and pecans to the air fryer container and air-broil for 4 minutes at 400°F, shaking the bushel once amid the cooking time.

- Exchange the grapes, fennel and pecans to a bowl with the kale. Dress the kale with the balsamic vinegar and olive oil, season to taste with salt and pepper and serve close by the cooked fish.

Chapter 7: Main Meals

Quinoa Burgers

These quinoa burgers are fulfilling and pack a punch of protein.

Ingredients

- 1 glass quinoa (red, white or multi-shaded)
- 1½ glasses water
- 1 teaspoon salt
- Naturally ground dark pepper
- 1½ glasses moved oats OR entire wheat breadcrumbs
- 3 eggs, gently beaten
- ¼ glass minced white onion
- ½ glass disintegrated feta cheddar
- ¼ glass cleaved new chives
- Salt and naturally ground dark pepper
- Vegetable or Canola oil
- Whole wheat ground sirloin sandwich buns
- Tomato piece
- Cucumber dill yogurt sauce

Guidelines

- Make the quinoa: Rinse the quinoa in icy water in a pot, twirling it with your hand until the point that any dry husks ascend to the surface. Deplete the quinoa and also you can and afterward put the pan on the stovetop. Turn the warmth to medium-between a rock and a hard place the quinoa on the stovetop, shaking the container routinely until the point when you see the quinoa moving effectively and can hear the seeds moving in the skillet. Include the water, salt and pepper. Heat the fluid to the point of boiling and afterward decrease the warmth to low or medium-low. You should simply observe a couple of air pockets, not a bubble. Cover with a top, abandoning it to one side (or on the off chance that you have pour gushes, simply put the top on the pot) and stew for 20 minutes. Subsidize the heat and cushion the quinoa with a fork. In the event that there's any fluid left in the base of the pot, put it back on the burner for an additional 3 minutes or somewhere in the vicinity. Spread the cooked quinoa out on a sheet skillet to cool.

- Conglomerate the room temperature quinoa in a huge bowl with the oats, eggs, onion, cheddar and herbs. Season with salt and pepper and amalgam well. Shape the blend into 4 patties. Include a little water or a couple of more moved oats to persuade the blend to be the correct consistency to make patties.

- Pre-warm a sauté container over medium warmth. Add enough oil to cover the base of the skillet. Add the quinoa burgers to the container. Cover and let the

CHAPTER 7: MAIN MEALS

burgers cook for 4 minutes. Check the base of the burger to ensure it has caramelized pleasantly. Flip the burger over, cover and cook for another 4 to 7 minutes, or until the point that the 2 sides are pleasantly sautéed.

- Air Fryer Instructions: Cascade the 2 sides of the patties liberally with oil and exchange them to the air fryer container in one layer (It is most likely that there will be need to cook these burgers in bunches relying upon the extent of the air fryer). Air-fry each group at 400°F for 10 minutes, flipping the burgers over part of the way through the cooking time.

- Make the burger all in all wheat ground sirloin sandwich buns with arugula, tomato and the cucumber dill yogurt sauce.

Air Fryer Drumsticks: Healthier Fried Chicken

It appears to be wrong that wings get the majority of the consideration when these Air Fryer Drumsticks are fit for an eatery banquet.

Grill nourishment gets a minor adjustment with an air fryer that prompts generous calorie investment funds and considerably more adjusted sustenance. The normal drumstick sees its wellbeing esteem decrease quickly, showered in oil, broiled and regularly bundled in a family-estimate basin no individual could vanquish. This air fryer recipe has your health opulence as a top priority, while additionally taking into account your most profound, darkest chicken longings. Cajun seasoning adds a pow of dramatization to this dish, which includes more satisfying meat on the bone than firm outside covering included.

Air Fryer Drumsticks are one Powerful with one Extra kick of astounding per serving. Appreciate them as seems to be, or pair them with a solid grain like darker rice for an awesome begin to a flex lunch.

Ingredients

- 2 chicken drumsticks, skin removed
- 2 tsp. olive oil
- 1 Tbsp. Cajun seasoning
- 1 Tbsp cayenne pepper
- 1 Tbsp paprika

CHAPTER 7: MAIN MEALS

- 1 Tbsp garlic powder

- 1 Tbsp onion powder

- 1 Tbsp oregano

Guidelines

- Consolidate olive oil and Cajun seasoning for marinade in an enclosed satchel.

- Include chicken and let it marinate for no less than 30 minutes.

- Preheat air fryer to 400° F.

- Exchange chicken to air fryer container and cook for another 15 minutes

Eggplant Parmesan Panini

There are a couple of ventures to making this Panini, yet it's justified, despite all the trouble at last. It takes every one of the kinds of Eggplant Parmesan and places it in a generous Panini! Salting eggplant before cooking may remove a chemical that tends to give eggplant an intense taste (there's much level headed discussion on this), however more critically it coaxes dampness out of the eggplant abandoning you with a lovelier and less stringy surface. Despite that it might appear to be disturbance to sprinkle a considerable measure of salt on the eggplant, rest guaranteed that you brush a large portion of the salt off the cuts previously cooking it, and your eggplant will be prepared flawlessly.

Ingredients

- 1 medium eggplant (around 1 pound), cut into ½-inch cuts
- Genuine salt
- ½ glass breadcrumbs
- 2 teaspoons dried parsley
- ½ teaspoon Italian flavoring
- ½ teaspoon garlic powder
- ½ teaspoon onion powder
- ½ teaspoon salt
- Crisply ground dark pepper

CHAPTER 7: MAIN MEALS

- 2 tablespoons drain
- ½ glass mayonnaise
- 4 cuts craftsman Italian bread
- ¾ glass tomato sauce
- 2 glasses ground mozzarella cheddar
- 2 tablespoons ground Parmesan cheddar or cheese
- Slashed crisp basil

Guidelines

- Set up the eggplant by liberally salting the 2 sides of the eggplant cuts and laying them level between sheets of paper towel. Give the eggplant a chance to sit like this for 30 minutes while you set up whatever is left of the formula ingredients.

- Set up anexcavating station. Consolidate the breadcrumbs, parsley, Italian flavoring, garlic powder, onion powder, salt and dark pepper in a shallow dish. Whisk the drain and mayonnaise together in a little bowl until smooth.

- Pre-warm the air fryer to 400°F.

- Brush the abundance salt from the eggplant cuts and afterward coats the 2 sides of each cut with the mayonnaise blend. Dunk the eggplant into the breadcrumbs, squeezing the morsels onto the eggplant to coat the 2 sides of each cut. Place all the covered eggplant cuts on a plate or preparing sheet and shower the 2 sides with olive oil. Air-fry the eggplant cuts in clusters for 14 minutes, turning them over part of the way through the cooking time.

- When the greater part of the eggplant has been fried, amass the Panini. Liberally brush 1 side of each cut of bread with olive oil. Place 2 cuts of bread on a cutting board, oiled side down. Top each cut with a 4th of the mozzarella cheddar and sprinkle with some Parmesan cheddar. Gap the cooked eggplant between the 2 Panini, putting them on the cheddar. Spoon the tomato sauce equitably finished the eggplant and best with residual mozzarella and Parmesan cheeses. Sprinkle with the hacked crisp basil and place the second cuts of bread to finish everything, oiled side up.

- Place sandwiches onto a pre-warmed contact barbecue or Panini press and close the cover, push down somewhat to ensure bread will dark colored equally. Flame broil for 10 minutes until the point that bread is toasted and cheddar is dissolved. On the other hand, flame broils the Panini in a barbecue dish with a Weighted push to finish everything and flip it over part of the way through cooking.

- Restore the completed cooked Panini to a cutting board and let them rest for 1 to 2 minutes. At that point, cut every down the middle and serve quickly.

CHAPTER 7: MAIN MEALS

Air Fryer Coconut Shrimp with Spicy Apricot Sauce

This fabulously sweet and crunchy formula is perfect for couples endeavoring to get fit as a fiddle by practicing good eating habits. Shrimp is a low-calorie type of protein you'll hunger for quite a long time when it's covered in tropically sweet coconut and made into crunchy bits of paradise in the air fryer. Avoid the rotisserie applications at the nearby bar, for a natively constructed take that beats its opposition anytime. Addicting doesn't start to portray this Air Fryer Coconut Shrimp, which is only 250 calories and, when utilizing precooked shrimp, is done in five minutes!

Since this great dish considers a large portion of a SmartCarb, one PowerFuel and two Extras, it is amazingly adaptable. Appreciate it as a between-feast nibble or as a base for a flex supper. In the event that you appreciate it as a flex nibble, don't hesitate to include a quarter measure of dark colored rice to round out the SmartCarb serving. On the off chance that you'd rather make it a flex supper, you can eat the two servings. Simply make sure to slice the sauce down the middle so you don't surpass your allocated additional items for the day.

Ingredients

- Coconut Shrimp
- 3 oz. peeled cooked shrimp
- 2 Tbsp. whole wheat flour
- ¼ cup shredded coconut, unsweetened

AIR FRYER COOKBOOK

- ¼ cup panko bread crumbs
- 1 egg, beaten
- Spicy Apricot Sauce
- 2 Tbsp. apricot preserves, sugar-free
- ½ tsp. light soy sauce
- 1 tsp. vinegar
- Pinch red pepper flakes

Guidelines:

- Preheat air fryer at 350 ° F.
- Get ready three dishes: one with flour, one with egg and one with the panko and coconut blended.
- Plunge shrimp into flour, at that point the egg, and afterward the coconut and panko blend.
- Place the covered shrimp into the sear bushel.
- Cook for 5 minutes (cooked shrimp) or 10 minutes (uncooked).
- Meanwhile, consolidate the greater part of the apricot sauce fixings in a little sauce container and mix it over medium warmth until the point when the jam is very much softened. Put aside and present with shrimp.

CHAPTER 7: MAIN MEALS

Apple Dumplings

Ingredients

- 2 very small apples
- 2 tablespoons raisins
- 1 tablespoon brown sugar
- 2 sheets puff pastry
- 2 tablespoons of melted butter

Guidelines

- Preheat your air fryer to 356°F.
- Core and peel the apples. Mix the raisins and the brown sugar.
- Put each apple on one of the puff pastry sheets then fill the core with the raisins and sugar. Fold the pastry around the apple so it is fully covered.
- Place the apple dumplings on a small sheet of foil (so if any juices escape they don't fall into the air fryer). Brush the dough with the melted butter.
- Place in you air fryer and set the timer to 25 minutes and bake the apple dumplings until golden brown and the apples are soft. Turn the apples over one time during cooking so that they will cook evenly.

Air Fried Mozzarella Sticks

A blend of Garlic powder, Italian seasoning, and simply enough Panko breadcrumbs to make the food delightfully firm, will make you select this recipe as your preferred top choice. On the off chance that the 99 calories for each serving still has you in dismay, allows simply say that air fryers are a grimy small abstaining from food mystery. This little, yet capable machine serves up all the wow factor related with a grand plate of mozzarella sticks in an essentially more advantageous way.

Ingredient

- 6 mozzarella string cheese sticks, low fat
- 1 cup Panko breadcrumbs, plain
- 1 large egg
- 1 Tbsp. Italian seasoning
- 1 tsp. garlic powder

Guidelines

- Preheat Air Fryer at 400° F.
- Beat the egg in a little bowl.
- Combine bread scraps, garlic powder and Italian seasoning.

CHAPTER 7: MAIN MEALS

- Plunge string cheddar into the bowl of egg and afterward coat with the breadcrumbs blend. Rehash for outstanding sticks of cheddar.

- Stop the sticks for 20-30 minutes.

- Air fry cheese sticks for 10 minutes, flipping most of the way for cooking.

AIR FRYER COOKBOOK

Philly Chicken Cheesesteak Stromboli

Ingredients

- ½ onions, Piece
- 1 teaspoon vegetable oil
- 2 boneless, skinless chicken bosoms, somewhat solidified and cut thin on the inclination (around 1 pound)
- 1 tablespoon of Worcestershire sauce
- Salt and crisply ground dark pepper
- 14ounces' pizza batter (locally acquired or natively constructed)
- 1½ container ground cheddar
- ½ container Cheese Whiz (or other bumped cheddar sauce), warmed delicately in the microwave

Guidelines

- Pre-warm the air fryer to 400°F.
- Hurl the cut onion with oil and air-fry for 8 minutes, mixing part of the way through the cooking time. Include the cut chicken and Worcestershire sauce to the air fryer basket, and hurl to equally disseminate the ingredients. Season the blend with salt and crisply ground dark pepper and air-broil for 8 minutes, mixing several times amid the cooking procedure. Expel the

CHAPTER 7: MAIN MEALS

chicken and onion from the air fryer and let the blend cool a bit.

- On a softly floured surface, roll or press the pizza batter out into a 13-inch by 11-inch rectangle, with the long side nearest to you. Sprinkle half of the cheddar over the batter leaving a vacant 1-inch outskirt from the edge most distant far from you. Top the cheddar with the chicken and onion blend, spreading it out uniformly. Shower the cheddar sauce over the meat and sprinkle the rest of the cheddar to finish everything.

- Begin rolling the Stromboli far from you and toward the vacant fringe. Ensure the filling remains firmly tucked inside the roll. At last, tuck the closures of the batter in and squeeze the crease close. Place the crease side down and shape the Stromboli into a U-shape to fit noticeable all around rotisserie bushel. Cut 4 little openings with the tip of a sharp blade uniformly in the highest point of the batter and softly brush the Stromboli with a little oil.

- Pre-warm the air fryer to 370°F.

- Splash or brush air fryer container with oil and exchange the U-molded Stromboli to the air fryer bushel. Air-fry to transform the Stromboli out of the air fryer basket and after that slide it again into the basket off the plate.)

- To evacuate painstakingly flip Stromboli over onto a cutting board. Allow it to cool for some minutes

75

previously serving. Cut the Stromboli into 3-inch pieces and present with ketchup for plummeting if wanted.

CHAPTER 7: MAIN MEALS

Air Fryer Frittata

Rather than wandering off in fantasy land about the informal breakfast nourishments your friends are getting a charge out of, create a light, protein-pressed and flavorful dinner that'll dispatch your day the correct way. Mushrooms, tomato and chive draw out the serious canons for plant new flavor to supplement feathery billows of egg white that needs no help from cheese.

Ingredients

- 1 cup egg whites
- 2 Tbsp. skim milk
- ¼ cup sliced tomato
- ¼ cup sliced mushrooms
- 2 Tbsp. chopped fresh chives
- Black pepper, to taste

Guidelines

- Preheat Air Fryer at 320° F.
- In a bowl, combine all the ingredients.
- Transfer to a greased frying pan (which may be provided with the air fryer) or to the bottom of the air fryer (after removing the accessory)
- Bake for 15 minutes or until frittata is cooked through

Roasted Vegetable Pasta Salad

This serviette of mixed greens incorporates the finish of summer vegetables yet cooked (or flame broiled first). Why would that be an awesome summer food? Since you can make it early – in reality it needs some time for the flavors to blend - abandoning you allowing something even better, which is, watch another person do the flame broiling!

Ingredients

- 1 orange pepper, huge piece
- 1 green pepper, huge piece
- 1 red pepper, huge piece
- 1 zucchini, cut down through the middle moons
- 1 yellow squash cut down the middle moons
- 1 red onion, piece
- 4 ounces dark colored mushrooms split
- 1 teaspoon Italian flavoring
- Salt and new ground dark pepper
- 1 pound of cooked penne rigatoni,
- 1 container grape tomatoes split
- ½ glasses set Kalamata olives, divided
- 3 tablespoons balsamic vinegar

CHAPTER 7: MAIN MEALS

- ¼ glass olive oil

- 2 tablespoons cleaved crisp basil

Guidelines

- Preheat the air fryer to 380°F.

- Place the peppers, zucchini, yellow squash, red onion and mushrooms in a substantial bowl, sprinkle with a tad bit of the olive oil and hurl to coat well. Include the Italian flavoring and season with salt and pepper. Air-fry for 12 to 14 minutes, until the point that the vegetables are delicate yet not soft. Mix or shake the container part of the way through the cooking time to uniformly broil vegetables.

- Consolidate the cooked pasta, broiled vegetables, tomatoes and olives in a substantial bowl and blend well. Include the balsamic vinegar and hurl. Add enough olive oil to coat everything pleasantly (you may not utilize everything). Season with salt and naturally ground dark pepper to taste.

- Refrigerate the plate of mixed greens until when you are prepared to serve. Mix in the crisp basil just before serving.

CHAPTER 8
DESSERTS AND SWEETS

Onion Rings

This recipe is one of the most effortless, yet most delectable bites to make utilizing an air fryer, all you require is to utilize the air searing method and this formula to get a similar outcome, yet significantly more beneficial.

Ingredients:

- 4 ounces of frozen battered onion rings
- onion rings air fryer recipe

Guidelines

- Add the onion rings into the frying basket of your air fryer.
- Once again, if there is a French fry setting available, choose it, since it delivers the result you want. The onion rings should fry for 10 minutes.
- After 10 minutes, remove the basket and toss the onion rings.
- Return it into the air fryer and repeat the cooking process for another 10 minutes.
- If you feel they aren't ready yet, you can cook them longer.
- Serve them with any preferred sauce

CHAPTER 8: DESSERTS AND SWEETS

Air Baked Molten Lava Cakes

Ingredients

- 1.5 TBS Self-rising Flour
- 3.5 TBS Baker's Sugar (Not Powdered)
- 3.5 OZ Unsalted Butter
- 3.5 OZ Dark Chocolate (Pieces or Chopped)
- 2 Eggs

Guidelines

- Preheat Your Air Fryer to 375F
- Grease and flour 4 standard oven safe ramekins.
- Melt dark chocolate and butter in a microwave safe bowl on level 7 for 3 minutes, stirring throughout. Remove from microwave and stir until even consistency.
- Whisk/Beat the eggs and sugar until pale and frothy.
- Pour melted chocolate mixture into egg mixture. Stir in flour. Use a spatula to combine everything evenly.
- Fill the ramekins about 3/4 full with cake mixture and bake in preheated air fryer at 375F for 10 minutes.
- Remove from the air fryer and allow to cool in ramekin for 2 minutes. Carefully turn ramekins upside down

AIR FRYER COOKBOOK

onto serving plate, tapping the bottom with a butter knife to loosen edges.

- Cake should release from ramekin with little effort and center should appear dark/gooey. Enjoy warm a-la-mode or with a raspberry drizzle.

CHAPTER 8: DESSERTS AND SWEETS

Apple Fries with Caramel Cream Dip

This is one delicious treat you'll get out of your air-fryer. The apples get warm and only somewhat delicate and delicate within, yet can hold there possess when you plunge them. You can likewise have a go at plunging into chocolate sauce or simply caramel sauce on the off chance that you need to keep it dairy free.

Ingredients

- 3 Pink Lady or Honey-crisp apples, peeled, cored and cut into 8 wedges
- ½ container flour
- 3 eggs, beaten
- 1 container graham wafer scraps
- ¼ container sugar
- 8 ounces whipped cream cheddar
- ½ container caramel sauce, in addition to additional for embellish

Guidelines

- Hurl the apple cuts and flour together in a substantial bowl. Set up a digging station by putting the beaten eggs in a single shallow dish, and consolidating the pounded graham wafers and sugar in a moment shallow dish. Plunge every apple cut into the egg, and after that

83

- into the graham saltine morsels. Coat the cuts on all sides and place the covered cuts on a treat sheet.

- Pre-warm the air fryer to 380°F. Shower or brush the base of the air fryer bushel with oil.

- Air-fry the apples in bunches. Place one layer of apple cuts noticeable all around fryer crate and shower delicately with oil. Air-fry for 4 minutes. Turn the apples over and air - fry for an extra 2 minutes.

- While apples are cooking influence caramel cream to plunge. Consolidate the whipped cream cheddar and caramel sauce, blending great. Exchange the Caramel Cream Dip into a serving dish and sprinkle extra caramel sauce over the best.

- Serve the apple fries hot with the caramel cream plunge as an afterthought!

CHAPTER 8: DESSERTS AND SWEETS

Air fryer Caramel Cheesecake

These are nearly nothing and charming and ideal for the Airfryer and they are simple to make.

Ingredients

- Hand Mixer
- Spring Form Pan
- Instant Pot
- 6 Digestives
- 50 g Melted Butter
- 1 Can Condensed Milk
- 500 g Soft Cheese
- 250 g Caster Sugar
- 4 Large Eggs
- 1 Tbsp Vanilla Essence
- 1 Tbsp Melted Chocolate

Guidelines

- In your Instant Pot place the can of condensed milk in it without its can wrappings submerged in water. Cook it for 40 minutes on manual and remember to seal it.
- Preheat the Airfryer to 180c.

- Flour the sides and bottom of your spring form pan with your hands so that it becomes non-stick.

- Crumble the digestive biscuits by giving it a hammering with a rolling pin inside a sandwich bag or inside its wrappers.

- Mix the melted butter into the crumbled digestives inside the spring form pan (less washing up that way) and using your hands make sure it pushes down on the bottom.

- In a mixing bowl and using a hand mixer, mix the sugar into the soft cheese until it is nice and fluffy. Add the eggs and vanilla essence and mix in with the mixer. Put to one side.

- When the condensed milk is done and cooled down, open it up and pour the caramel into the bowl. Mix it in with a fork and then place the mixture into the spring form pan over the biscuit base.

- Level it and make it smooth with the spatula.

- Cook for 15 minutes at 180c, 10 minutes at 160c and then a last 15 minutes at 150c.

- When it is done, place it in the fridge to cool for 6 hours.

- Drizzle over the top with fork small amounts of melted chocolate and leftover caramel when done.

CHAPTER 8: DESSERTS AND SWEETS

Air Fried Sugared Dough Dippers with Chocolate Amaretto Sauce

It has never been this easy! If you have purchase bread or pizza batter, you should simply roll and air fry!

Ingredients

- 1 pound of bread batter, defrosted
- ½ dissolved cup spread butter
- ¾ to 1 container of sugar
- 1 container overwhelming cream
- 12ounces of quality semi-sweet chocolate chips
- 2 tablespoons Amaretto alcohol (or almond extricate)

Guidelines

- Roll the batter into 2¼-inch logs. Cut each sign into 20 cuts. Cut each cut down the middle and bend the batter parts together 3 to 4 times. Place the contorted batter on a treat sheet, brush with softened margarine and sprinkle sugar over the mixture turns.

- Pre-warm the air fryer to 340°F.

- Brush the base of the air fryer crate with liquefied spread. Air-fry the mixture winds in bunches. Place 8 to 12 (contingent upon the span of your air fryer) noticeable all around fryer basket.

- Air-fry for 4 minutes. Turn the mixture strips over and brush the opposite favor margarine. Air-fry for an extra 3 minutes.

- While batter is cooking, influence the chocolate amaretto to sauce. Convey the overwhelming cream to a stew over medium warmth. Place the chocolate contributes an expansive bowl and pour the hot cream over the chocolate chips. Blend until the point that the chocolate begins to liquefy. At that point change to a wire whisk and race until the point when the chocolate is totally liquefied and the sauce is smooth. Blend in the Amaretto. Exchange to a serving dish.

- As the clusters of batter turns are finished, put them into a shallow dish. Brush with softened margarine and liberally coat with sugar, shaking the dish to cover the 2 sides.

- Serve the sugared mixture scoops with the warm chocolate Amaretto sauce as an addendum.

CHAPTER 8: DESSERTS AND SWEETS

Crispy Fried Spring Rolls

The disparitiesin hot air fryer recipes are quite much, but this recipe in adapts to the air frying technique

Ingredients

- 120g cooked chicken breast
- 1 celery stalk
- 30 g carrot
- 30 g mushrooms
- ½ tsp finely chopped ginger
- 1 tsp sugar
- 1 tsp chicken stock powder
- 1 egg
- 1 tsp corn starch
- 8 spring roll wrappers

Guidelines

- Tear the cooked chicken breasts into shreds. Slice the celery, carrot and mushroom into long thin strips.

- Place the shredded chicken into a bowl and mix with the celery, carrot and mushroom. Add the ginger, sugar and chicken stock powder and stir evenly to make the spring roll filling.

- Whisk the egg, and then add the corn starch and mix to create a thick paste. Set aside.

- Place some filling onto each spring roll wrapper and roll it up, then seal the ends with the egg mixture. For a crispy result, lightly brush the spring rolls with oil.

- Preheat the Airfryer to 200°C.

- Place the rolls into the Airfryer basket and slide the basket into the Airfryer. Set the timer for 4 minutes. Serve with sweet chill sauce

CHAPTER 8: DESSERTS AND SWEETS

Midnight Nutella Banana Sandwich

These debauched basic treats are an immaculate midnight nibble and are particularly great with a little nip of Grand Marnier. You can make numerous minor departure from this sandwich by substituting different elements for the bananas – attempt raspberries, strawberries or even cuts of ready peach.

Ingredients

- Mollified Butter,
- 4 pieces of white bread
- ¼ container chocolate hazelnut spread (Nutella®)
- 1 banana

Guidelines

- Pre-warm the air fryer to 370°F.
- Spread the mollified margarine on 1 side of the considerable number of cuts of bread and place the cuts, buttered side down on the counter. Spread the chocolate hazelnut spread on the opposite side of the bread cuts. Cut the banana down the middle and after that cut every half into 3 cuts the long way. Place the banana cuts on 2 cuts of bread and best with the rest of the cuts of bread to make 2 sandwiches. Cut the sandwiches down the middle (triangles or rectangles) – this will help them all fit noticeable all around fryer on the double. Exchange the sandwiches to the air fryer.

- Air-fry at 370°F for 4 minutes. Flip the sandwiches over and air-broil for another 2 to 3 minutes or until the point when the best bread cuts are pleasantly cooked. Present yourself with a glass of drain or a midnight nightcap while the sandwiches cool and then enjoy!

CHAPTER 8: DESSERTS AND SWEETS

Blueberry Cheesecake

This particular one is stunning in light of the fact that you can enrich it as you wish and after that take it to a birthday party, a dedicating, a child shower or for a cookout on the shoreline

Ingredients

- Spring Form Pan
- 6 Digestives
- 50 g Melted Butter
- 600 g Soft Cheese
- 300 g Caster Sugar
- 4 Large Eggs
- 100 g Fresh Blueberries
- 2 Tbsp Greek Yoghurt
- 1 Tbsp Vanilla Essence
- 5 Tbsp Icing Sugar

Guidelines

- Preheat your Airfryer to 180c.
- Flour the sides and bottom of your spring form pan so that when you cook your cheesecake that it won't stick.

- Crumble the digestive biscuits and mix them with the melted butter. Push them down into the bottom of the spring form pan so that they form the base.

- Cream the cheese and the sugar together with a hand mixer until they are light but incredibly thick and fluffy.

- Add the eggs (one at a time), the Greek Yoghurt, vanilla essence and mix everything as you put it in.

- Chop the blueberries into quarters. Place a quarter of them into the soft cheese mixture and mix well.

- Using a big spoon (I used a soup spoon) spoon the mixture into the spring form pan and use a spatula to flatten any bubbles and to give it a very smooth feeling.

- Place in the Airfryer and cook at 180c for 15 minutes, 160c for 10 minutes and then a further 15 minutes at 150c. This will ensure that it cooked everywhere and not just on the top.

- When the Airfryer beeps, place it into the fridge and allow cooling for 12 hours.

- Once cooled take the rest of the blueberries and cook them in a pan with a little icing sugar and once they are melted down to half their size, spoon over the cheesecake for the top layer.

- Serve.

CHAPTER 8: DESSERTS AND SWEETS

Birthday Cake Cheesecake

Add some crisp blueberries to your cheesecake and you can have a delightful summer cheesecake. It doesn't require as long in the cooler to set.

Ingredients

- Airfryer
- Hand Mixer
- Spring Form Pan
- 6 Digestives
- 50 g Melted Butter
- 800 g Soft Cheese
- 500 g Caster Sugar
- 4 Tbsp Cocoa Powder
- 6 Large Eggs
- 2 Tbsp Honey
- 1 Tbsp Vanilla Essence
- Melted Chocolate

Guidelines

- Flour the bottom and sides of a spring form pan so that it no longer sticks.

- Bash your digestive biscuits inside a sandwich bag with a rolling pin until they resemble breadcrumbs. Mix into them the melted butter and then push them down into the bottom of your spring form pan.

- In a mixing bowl mix together the soft cheese and caster sugar with a hand mix. Add to it 5 out of 6 of the eggs, honey and vanilla essence and mix with the hand mixer until everything is well mixed in.

- Using a large spoon, spoon half of it into the spring form pan over the crumbly base. Pat it down with a spatula and get rid of any lumps and bumps. Place the rest of the mixture into the fridge.

- Cook it at 180c for 20 minutes, 15 minutes at 160c and then a final 20 minutes at 150c. Transfer it to the fridge and allow to set for a further hour.

- After an hour, get the rest of the mixture out of the fridge. Crack in the final egg and the cocoa powder and give it a good mix with a fork.

- Spoon it over the set bottom cheesecake layer and return to the fridge for 11 hours.

- After it has been resting decorate it as you please. Splash melted chocolate over the sides, add lots of chocolate pieces or however you see fit depending on the occasion.

- Serve.

CHAPTER 8: DESSERTS AND SWEETS

Fried Hot Prawns with Cocktail Sauce

Ingredients:

- 8-12 fresh king prawns
- 1 tbsp of cider or wine vinegar
- 3 tbsp of mayonnaise
- 1 tbsp of ketchup
- 1 tsp chili flakes
- 1/2 tsp of sea salt
- 1/2 tsp of freshly ground black pepper
- 1 tsp of chili powder

Guidelines

- Preheat your air fryer to 180°C.
- To season the prawns, mix all the spices in a bowl.
- After doing so, add the prawns and mix them well with all the seasonings.
- Once seasoned, the prawns are ready for frying.
- Place the prawns into the frying basket, and return the basket into the air fryer.

AIR FRYER COOKBOOK

- These prawns should be cooked for 6 to 8 minutes, so adjust the timer accordingly. The frying time depends on the size of the prawns.

- The remaining ingredients from the list should be used for the cocktail sauce.

- Mix them together and serve the fried prawns with it.

- After you taste this dish, it will definitely be among the best air fryer recipes for you

CHAPTER 9
SOUP

Asian Shrimp Noodle Soup

Ingredients

- 24 vast shrimp, unpeeled
- 4 mugs vegetable stock
- 1 tablespoon of vegetable oil
- 1 red onion, cut
- 2 carrots, cut into julienne strips
- 2 ribs celery, cut on the inclination ¼" thick
- 2minced cloves garlic,
- 2 tablespoons ground crisp ginger
- ½ - 1 red bean stew pepper, divided
- 2 (14-ounce) jars coconut drain
- ½ pound rice vermicelli noodles
- 1 tablespoon of soy sauce
- 3pieces of scallions,
- ¼ glass new cilantro clears out

AIR FRYER COOKBOOK

- 1 lime, cut into chunks

Guidelines

- Peel and devein the shrimp, holding the shells. Put the peeled shrimp aside. Consolidate the vegetable stock and held shrimp shells in a pot. Stew together for 30 minutes. At that point strain out and dispose of the shrimp shells, saving the capital.

- Heat a stockpot or Dutch oven over medium warmth. Include the vegetable oil and daintily sauté the onion, carrot, and celery until delicate – around 6 to 8 minutes. Include the garlic, ginger, bean stew pepper parts and cook for 1 to 2 minutes. Include the saved vegetable stock and coconut drain, and convey to a stew. Stew for 20 minutes.

- In the meantime, in a different bowl or pot, pour bubbling water over the rice noodles and let them sit while the soup stews.

- Deplete and add the noodles to the soup, alongside the shrimp, soy sauce, and scallions. Stew just until the point when the shrimp is pink and obscure – around 2 to 4 minutes. Include the cilantro and present with the lime wedges.

CHAPTER 9: SOUP

Basic Chicken Noodle Soup

Hardly is any other thing are as improving as a bowl of chicken noodle soup. This fundamental form never neglects to fulfill and is significantly less demanding to make than you might suspect

Ingredients

- 1 tablespoon olive oil
- 1 onion, finely chopped
- 2finely slashed carrots,
- 2 ribs celery finely cut
- 2 cloves garlic, finely slashed
- ½ teaspoon dried thyme
- 1 inlet leaf
- 2 quarts' great quality or hand-crafted chicken or vegetable stock
- 3 containers cooked chicken, destroyed or cut into chomp estimated pieces
- 1½ mugsextensive egg noodles salt, to taste newly ground dark pepper
- ¼ container hacked new parsley

AIR FRYER COOKBOOK

Guidelines

- Heat a stockpot or Dutch stove over medium fire. Include the olive oil and delicately sauté the onion, carrot, and celery until delicate – around 6 to 8 minutes.

- Include the garlic, thyme and inlet leaf and cook for one more minute.

- Include the chicken stock, and convey to a stew. Stew for 20 minutes.

- Include the cooked chicken and noodles in the pot and cook until the point when noodles are still somewhat firm – 6 to 8 minutes.

- Purge the straight leaf from the soup, season with salt and pepper, include parsley and serve quickly

CHAPTER 9: SOUP

Curried Sweet Potato Soup

Ingredients

- 2 tablespoons of butter
- 1 tablespoon olive oil
- ½ onion, hacked (about ½ glass)
- 4 to 6 sweet potatoes, peeled and diced
- 1 tablespoon of curry powder
- 4 containers chicken stock, vegetable stock or water
- ¾ container squeezed orange
- ½ teaspoon salt or more to taste newly ground dark pepper
- ½ container harsh cream (discretionary)
- 3 tablespoons of hacked crisp parsley

Guidelines

- Dissolve the margarine alongside the olive oil in a stockpot or Dutch stove over medium warmth.
- Include the onion and cook for 4 to 7 minutes. The onion ought to be translucent, not darker.
- Include the sweet potatoes and curry powder, and keep on cooking for another 6 to 8 minutes.

- Include the chicken stock, vegetable stock or water and keep on simmering for an additional 20 minutes. Mix in the squeezed orange.

- Utilizing a blender, sustenance processor, nourishment factory or inundation blender, puree the soup until the point that no knots remain and the soup is smooth.

- Restore the soup to the stovetop and thin the soup with water until you've achieved the coveted consistency.

- Include salt and naturally ground dark pepper.

- Present with a bit of sour cream and cleaved parsley to embellish.

CHAPTER 9: SOUP

Tuscan Chicken and White Bean Soup

This soup is flavorful and simple to make. It will warm and top you off!

Ingredients

- 4ounces' pancetta (or bacon on the off chance that you can't discover pancetta)
- 1 onion, finely diced
- 3minced cloves garlic,
- 1 teaspoon dried thyme
- 1 teaspoon dried basil
- ½ teaspoon dried rosemary
- 2 tablespoons tomato glue
- 3 containers chicken stock
- 1 (28-ounce) tomatoes
- 2 glasses destroyed, cooked chicken
- 2 (14-ounce) jars white cannellini beans, depleted and flushed
- 4 pieces ciabatta rolls or 1 ciabatta baguette,
- Olive oil
- 4 ounces crisp infant spinach, cleaned

- 1 teaspoon salt
- Naturally ground dark pepper
- Square of Parmesan cheese

Guidelines

- Place pancetta in an expansive stockpot and cook until the point when a portion of the fat has been rendered out – around 6 to 8 minutes.

- Expel the pancetta with an opened spoon and put it aside.

- Add the onion to the stockpot and cook until the point when the onion begins to relax – around 6 minutes.

- Include the garlic, thyme, basil, rosemary and tomato glue, mix to mix well, and cook for one more moment or 2. Include the chicken stock, tomatoes, destroyed chicken and beans to the pot and blend well.

- Stew the soup for 30 minutes. While the soup is stewing, pre-warm a skillet over medium warmth.

- Include olive oil and toast the cut side of the ciabatta rolls or cuts in the skillet until pleasantly cooked.

- Exorcize the soup from the excess heat and mix in the spinach. Season to taste with salt and pepper.

- Serve the soup with a portion of the cooked pancetta sprinkled to finish everything, a few shards of

CHAPTER 9: SOUP

Parmesan cheddar (made by peeling the cheddar with a potato peeler) and the toasted ciabatta bread.